A BOOK OF VERSE
FOR CHILDREN

PARTS I–III

*The complete book
contains Five Parts*

A
BOOK OF VERSE
FOR CHILDREN

Compiled by

ALYS RODGERS, L.L.A.(Hons.)

PARTS I-III

Cambridge:
at the University Press
1914

CAMBRIDGE
UNIVERSITY PRESS

University Printing House, Cambridge CB2 8BS, United Kingdom

Cambridge University Press is part of the University of Cambridge.

It furthers the University's mission by disseminating knowledge in the pursuit of
education, learning and research at the highest international levels of excellence.

www.cambridge.org
Information on this title: www.cambridge.org/9781107487246

© Cambridge University Press 1914

First published 1914
First paperback edition 2015

A catalogue record for this publication is available from the British Library

ISBN 978-1-107-48724-6 Paperback

PREFATORY NOTE

THE following anthology of children's poems aims, in the first place, at supplying a want felt in both secondary and elementary schools, where pieces for recitation and general reading are essential for the kindergarten and first form departments; and, secondly, at providing a collection of verses for out-of-school enjoyment. The first three parts, together with the first half of the fourth part, form a carefully-graduated course—mainly consisting of nature poems—for very young children; while the remainder of the book is intended to secure a similar purpose for children of rather higher literary attainments.

The compiler desires to record her grateful thanks for much help and information, also for courteous permission to include the following copyright works in this collection of children's poems; she also begs for kind indulgence from the authors and publishers of any poems, which, in spite of much diligence, she has been unable to trace to their original place of publication.

The Earl of Crewe kindly gave consent for *The Moon* by Lord Houghton : Miss L. I. Guiney for the *Carol :* Mr R. C. Lehmann and Messrs Blackwood and Sons for *On Saturday Morning Early :* Madame Duclaux for *Sir Hugh and the Swans :* Mr G. F. Bradby for *The Flowing Tide :* the Rev. Conrad Noel for *The Water-Nymph and the Boy* by the Hon. R. Noel : Mrs K. Tynan-Hinkson for *Sheep and Lambs :* the Rev. Garrett Horder for *An Evening Hymn* by Miss Betham-Edwards : Mrs Allingham for *The Fairies* and *Wishing* by the late Mr W. Allingham : the Earl of Meath for *The Children's Song* by Mr Rudyard Kipling : Mr Theodore Watts-Dunton and Messrs Chatto & Windus for Swinburne's *In a Garden :* Mr Henry Newbolt for *Hawke* and *Gillespie :* Messrs Longmans, Green and Co. gave kind permission to reprint five poems from *A Child's Garden of Verse* by R. L. Stevenson : Mr T. Fisher Unwin for *Father Gilligan* by Mr W. B. Yeats : Messrs Chatto and Windus for eight poems by Dr George Macdonald : the Rev. Canon Beeching for *Going Down Hill on a Bicycle :* Sir Gilbert Parker for *Little Garaine :* Mr Elkin Matthews for *The Witches' Steeds* by Mr W. H. Ogilvie : Mr John Lane for five of Mr Eugene Field's poems, and *The Pedlar's Caravan* by Mr W. B. Rands : Messrs

Macmillan and Co. for the *Christmas Carol* by Christina Rossetti, and *The Prayers* by T. E. Brown : Mr William Watson and Mr John Lane for *Song:* Messrs Parker and Co. for *The Song of the Western Men,* taken from Hawker's *Cornish Ballads :* and Mr W. Heinemann for Björnson's *The Tree.*

A. R.

February 1914

CONTENTS

PART I

		PAGE
1. A Child's Grace	R. Herrick	1
2. The Selkirk Grace	R. Burns	1
3. Baby	G. Macdonald	1
4. My Little Brother	M. L. Duncan	3
5. Bed in Summer	R. L. Stevenson	4
6. Oh ! Look at the Moon	E. L. Follen	4
7. The Old Kitchen Clock	Mrs Hawkshawe	5
8. Cradle Song	Lord Tennyson	6
9. Dutch Lullaby	Eugene Field	7
10. Sweet and Low	Lord Tennyson	9
11. Letty's Globe	C. Tennyson-Turner	10
12. In a Garden	A. C. Swinburne	11
13. Norse Lullaby	Eugene Field	12
14. The Land of Nod	R. L. Stevenson	13
15. Lullaby of an Infant Chief	Sir W. Scott	14
16. The Days are Cold	D. Wordsworth	15
17. A Sleeping Child	A. H. Clough	15
18. Bed-Time	T. Hood	17
19. The Land of Story Books	R. L. Stevenson	18
20. Babyland	G. Cooper	19
21. Wishing	W. Allingham	20
22. The Pedlar's Caravan	W. B. Rands	21
23. A Lobster Quadrille	Lewis Carroll	22

			PAGE
24.	The Cherry Tree	*R. L. Stevenson*	24
25.	Seven Times One	*J. Ingelow*	25
26.	Valentine's Day	*C. Kingsley*	26
27.	The Fairies	*W. Allingham*	27
28.	My Treasures	*R. L. Stevenson*	29

PART II

1.	A Charm	*R. Herrick*	31
2.	A Riddle	*G. Macdonald*	31
3.	The Curfew	*H. W. Longfellow*	32
4.	The Moon	*Lord Houghton*	33
5.	The Lamb	*W. Blake*	34
6.	The World	*W. B. Rands*	34
7.	The Daisy's Song	*J. Keats*	35
8.	Little Garaine	*Sir Gilbert Parker*	36
9.	Written in March	*W. Wordsworth*	37
10.	Buttercups and Daisies	*M. Howitt*	38
11.	To a Bee	*R. Southey*	40
12.	The Lady-Bird	*Mrs Montgomery*	41
13.	Song from *The Water Babies*	*C. Kingsley*	42
14.	The Blackbird	*Lord Tennyson*	42
15.	The Owl	*Lord Tennyson*	43
16.	The Land of Dreams	*W. Blake*	44
17.	On Saturday Morning Early	*R. C. Lehmann*	45
18.	Song	*W. Watson*	48
19.	The Witches' Steeds	*W. H. Ogilvie*	48
20.	Daffy-Down-Dilly	*A. B. Warner*	49
21.	Heigho, My Dearie	*Eugene Field*	51

			PAGE
22.	Three Men of Gotham	*T. L. Peacock*	53
23.	March	*L. Larcom*	54
24.	Hie Away	*Sir W. Scott*	55
25.	The Water! The Water!	*W. Motherwell*	55
26.	The Rivulet	*L. Larcom*	56
27.	The Ant	*I. Watts*	58
28.	Little Ships in the Air	*E. A. Rand*	59
29.	The Flowers	*W. B. Rands*	60
30.	Answer to a Child's Question	*S. T. Coleridge*	61
31.	Over the Hills and Far Away	*Eugene Field*	62
32.	What way does the Wind come?	*D. Wordsworth*	63
33.	A Tragic Story	*W. M. Thackeray*	65
34.	The Wind and the Moon	*G. Macdonald*	66
35.	The Wind in a Frolic	*W. Howitt*	69

PART III

1.	A Ceremony for Candlemas Day	*R. Herrick*	72
2.	The Year's at the Spring	*R. Browning*	72
3.	The Morning	*A. Cunningham*	73
4.	The Fountain	*J. R. Lowell*	74
5.	The Shepherd	*W. Blake*	76
6.	The First Sight of Spring	*J. Clare*	76
7.	Green Fields of England	*A. H. Clough*	77
8.	The Tree	*B. Björnson*	78
9	May	*Leigh Hunt*	79
10.	Impromptu	*W. Wordsworth*	80
11.	The Procession of the Flowers	*S. Dobell*	81
12.	The Housekeeper	*O. Lamb*	82

			PAGE
13.	The Sea	*Barry Cornwall*	83
14.	Up, Up! Ye Dames and Lasses Gay!	*S. T. Coleridge*	84
15.	Fairy Language	*W. Shakespeare*	85
16.	Fairy Song	*J. Keats*	86
17.	The Fairy Queen	*Anonymous*	87
18.	When Green Leaves Come Again	*T. H. Bayly*	89
19.	Fairies' Recall	*F. D. Hemans*	90
20.	Flowers	*H. W. Longfellow*	91
21.	A Field Flower	*J. Montgomery*	92
22.	The Foolish Harebell	*G. Macdonald*	93
23.	Lilies	*Leigh Hunt*	96
24.	The Rose	*W. Cowper*	96
25.	The Violet	*J. Taylor*	97
26.	The Little Thirsty Lily	*G. Macdonald*	98
27.	The Arrow and the Song	*H. W. Longfellow*	100
28.	The Dog and the Water-Lily	*W. Cowper*	101
29.	Eldorado	*E. A. Poe*	103
30.	Lilian	*Lord Tennyson*	104
31.	The Mermaid	*Lord Tennyson*	105
32.	The Merman	*Lord Tennyson*	106
33.	I had a Dove	*J. Keats*	108
34.	Long Ago	*Eugene Field*	109
35.	If I had but Two Little Wings	*S. T. Coleridge*	110
36.	The Water-Nymph and the Boy	*Hon. R. Noel*	111
37.	The Night Bird	*C. Kingsley*	113
38.	Let Me Rest	*E. Elliot*	114
39.	Hiawatha's Childhood	*H. W. Longfellow*	115

PART I

1. A Child's Grace

Here a little child I stand
Heaving up my either hand.
Cold as Paddocks[1] though they be
Here I lift them up to Thee,
For a Benizon[2] to fall
On our meat, and on us all.

R. Herrick

2. The Selkirk Grace

Some hae meat, and canna eat,
　　And some wad eat that want it ;
But we hae meat, and we can eat,
　　And sae the Lord be thanket.

R. Burns

3. Baby

Where did you come from, baby dear ?
Out of the everywhere into here.

Where did you get those eyes so blue ?
Out of the sky as I came through.

---

[1] *Paddocks.* Frogs.　　　[2] *Benizon.* Blessing.

What makes the light in them sparkle and
    spin ?
Some of the starry twinkles left in.

Where did you get that little tear ?
I found it waiting when I got here.

What makes your forehead so smooth and
    high ?
A soft hand stroked it as I went by.

What makes your cheek like a warm white
    rose ?
I saw something better than anyone knows.

Whence that three-cornered smile of bliss ?
Three angels gave me at once a kiss.

Where did you get this pearly ear ?
God spoke, and it came out to hear.

Where did you get those arms and hands ?
Love made itself into bonds and bands.

Feet, whence did you come, you darling
    things ?
From the same box as the cherub's wings.

How did they all just come to be you ?
God thought about me, and so I grew.

But how did you come to us, you dear ?
God thought about you, and so I am here.

G. MACDONALD

4. MY LITTLE BROTHER

Little brother, darling boy,
   You are very dear to me !
I am happy—full of joy,
   When your smiling face I see.

How I wish that you could speak,
   And could know the words I say !
Pretty stories I would seek
   To amuse you every day.

All about the honey-bees,
   Flying past us in the sun ;
Birds that sing among the trees,
   Lambs that in the meadows run.

Shake your rattle—here it is,
   Listen to its merry noise ;
And, when you are tired of this,
   I will bring you other toys.

M. L. DUNCAN

5. Bed in Summer

In winter I get up at night
And dress by yellow candle-light.
In summer, quite the other way,
I have to go to bed by day.

I have to go to bed and see
The birds still hopping on the tree,
Or hear the grown-up people's feet
Still going past me in the street.

And does it not seem hard to you,
When all the sky is clear and blue,
And I should like so much to play,
To have to go to bed by day ?

R. L. Stevenson

6. Oh ! Look at the Moon

Oh ! Look at the moon,
  She is shining up there ;
Oh ! mother, she looks
  Like a lamp in the air.

Last week she was smaller,
  And shaped like a bow ;
But now she's grown bigger,
  And round as an O.

Pretty moon, pretty moon,
  How you shine on the door,
And make it all bright
  On my nursery floor !

You shine on my playthings,
  And show me their place,
And I love to look up
  At your pretty bright face.

And there is a star
  Close by you, and may be
That small twinkling star
  Is your little baby.
                    E. L. FOLLEN

7. THE OLD KITCHEN CLOCK

Listen to the kitchen clock !
  To itself it ever talks,
  From its place it never walks ;
" Tick-tock—tick-tock ! "
  Tell me what it says.

" I'm a very patient clock,
  Never moved by hope or fear,
  Though I've stood for many a year ;
Tick-tock—tick-tock ! "
  That is what it says.

" I'm a very truthful clock :
   People say about the place,
   Truth is written on my face ;
Tick-tock—tick-tock ! "
   That is what it says.

" I'm a very active clock,
   For I go while you're asleep,
   Though you never take a peep ;
Tick-tock—tick-tock ! "
   That is what it says.

" I'm a most obliging clock :
   If you wish to hear me strike,
   You may do it when you like ;
Tick-tock—tick-tock ! "
   That is what it says.

What a talkative old clock !
   Let us see what it will do
   When the pointer reaches two ;
" Ding-ding !   Tick-tock ! "
   That is what it says.
                               Mrs Hawkshawe

8. Cradle Song

What does little birdie say
In her nest at peep of day ?
" Let me fly," says little birdie,
" Mother, let me fly away."

Birdie, rest a little longer,
Till the little wings are stronger.
So she rests a little longer,
Then she flies away.

What does little baby say,
In her bed at peep of day ?
Baby says, like little birdie,
" Let me rise and fly away."
Baby, sleep a little longer,
Till the little limbs are stronger.
If she sleeps a little longer
Baby too shall fly away.

LORD TENNYSON

9. DUTCH LULLABY

Wynken, Blynken and Nod one night
   Sailed off in a wooden shoe—
Sailed on a river of misty light
   Into a sea of dew.
" Where are you going and what do you
     wish ? "
   The old moon asked the three.
" We have come to fish for the herring fish
   That live in this beautiful sea ;
   Nets of silver and gold have we,"
        Said Wynken,
        Blynken
        And Nod.

The old moon laughed and sang a song,
  As they rocked in the wooden shoe,
And the wind that sped them all night along
  Ruffled the waves of dew ;
The little stars were the herring fish
  That lived in the beautiful sea.
" Now cast your nets wherever you wish,
  But never afeared are we ! "
  So cried the stars to the fishermen three ;
      Wynken,
      Blynken,
      And Nod.

All night long their nets they threw
  For the fish in the twinkling foam ;
Then down from the sky came the wooden
    shoe,
  Bringing the fishermen home ;
'Twas all so pretty—a sail, it seemed
  As if it could not be ;
And some folk thought 'twas a dream they
    dreamed
  Of sailing that beautiful sea ;
  But I shall name you the fishermen three ;
      Wynken,
      Blynken,
      And Nod.

Wynken and Blynken are two little eyes.
  And Nod is a little head,

And the wooden shoe that sailed the skies
   Is a wee one's trundle-bed.[1]
So shut your eyes while mother sings
   Of wonderful sights that be,
And you shall see the beautiful things
   As you rock on the misty sea
   Where the old sea rocked the fishermen
     three ;
     Wynken,
     Blynken,
     And Nod.

               EUGENE FIELD

10. SWEET AND LOW

Sweet and low, sweet and low,
   Wind of the western sea,
Low, low, breathe and blow,
   Wind of the western sea !
Over the rolling waters go,
Come from the dying moon, and blow,
   Blow him again to me ;
While my little one, while my pretty one,
sleeps.

   Sleep and rest, sleep and rest,
     Father will come to thee soon ;
   Rest, rest, on mother's breast,
     Father will come to thee soon ;

[1] *Trundle,* or *truckle-bed.* A low bed on wheels, which may be pushed under an ordinary bed.

Father will come to his babe in the nest,
Silver sails all out of the west
    Under the silver moon :
Sleep, my little one, sleep, my pretty one,
  sleep.

LORD TENNYSON

11. LETTY'S GLOBE

When Letty had scarce pass'd her third glad
    year
And her young artless words began to flow.
One day we gave the child a colour'd sphere
Of the wide earth, that she might mark and
    know
By tint and outline, all its sea and land.
She patted all the world ; old empires peep'd
Between her baby fingers, her soft hand
Was welcome at all frontiers.   How she leap'd
And laugh'd and prattled in her world-wide
    bliss ;
But when we turned her sweet unlearnèd eye
On our own isle, she raised a joyous cry—
" Oh ! yes, I see it. Letty's home is there ! "
And while she hid all England with a kiss,
Bright over Europe fell her golden hair.

C. TENNYSON-TURNER

12. In a Garden

Baby, see the flowers !
    Baby sees
Fairer things than these,
Fairer though they be than dreams of ours.

    Baby, hear the birds !
      Baby knows
    Better songs than those,
Sweeter though they sound than sweetest
    words.

    Baby, see the moon !
      Baby's eyes
    Laugh to watch it rise
Answering light with love and night with noon.

    Baby, hear the sea !
      Baby's face
    Takes a graver grace,
Touched with wonder what the sound may be.

    Baby, see the star !
      Baby's hand
    Opens, warm and bland,
Calm in claim of all things fair that are.

    Baby, hear the bells !
      Baby's head

Bows as ripe for bed,
Now the flowers curl round and close their
  cells.

　Baby, flower of light,
　　Sleep and see
　Brighter dreams than we,
Till good day shall smile away good night.
　　　　　　　　A. C. SWINBURNE

13. NORSE LULLABY

The sky is dark and the hills are white
As the storm-king speeds from the north
  to-night ;
And this is the song the storm-king sings,
As over the world his cloak he flings :
　" Sleep, sleep, little one, sleep ; "
He rustles his wings and gruffly sings :
　" Sleep, little one, sleep."

On yonder mountain-side a vine
Clings at the foot of a mother pine ;
The tree bends over the trembling thing,
And only the vine can hear her sing :
　" Sleep, sleep, little one, sleep—
What shall you fear when I am here ?
　Sleep, little one, sleep."

The king may sing in his bitter flight,
The tree may croon to the vine to-night,
But the little snow-flake at my breast
Liketh the song *I* sing best.

   Sleep, sleep, little one, sleep ;
Weary thou art, a-next my heart;
   Sleep, little one, sleep.

EUGENE FIELD

14. THE LAND OF NOD

From breakfast on through all the day
At home among my friends I stay ;
But every night I go abroad
Afar into the Land of Nod.

All by myself I have to go,
With none to tell me what to do—
All alone beside the streams
And up the mountain-sides of dreams.

The strangest things are there for me,
Both things to eat and things to see,
And many frightening sights abroad
Till morning in the Land of Nod.

Try as I like to find the way,
I never can get back by day,
Nor can remember plain and clear
The curious music that I hear.

R. L. STEVENSON

15. LULLABY OF AN INFANT CHIEF

Oh, hush thee, my baby ! Thy sire was a
    knight,
Thy mother a lady, both lovely and bright ;
The woods and the glens, from the towers
    which we see,
They all are belonging, dear baby, to thee.

Oh, fear not the bugle, though loudly it blows !
It calls but the warders that guard thy repose ;
Their bows would be bended, their blades
    would be red,
'Ere the step of a foeman draws near to thy
    bed.

Oh, hush thee, my baby ! The time will soon
    come
When thy sleep shall be broken by trumpet
    and drum ;
Then hush thee, my darling ! Take rest while
    you may :
For strife comes with manhood, and waking
    with day.

SIR W. SCOTT

16. The Days are Cold

The days are cold, the nights are long,
The north-wind sings a doleful song ;
Then hush again upon my breast ;
All merry things are now at rest,
   Save thee, my pretty love !

The kitten sleeps upon the hearth,
The crickets long have ceased their mirth ;
There's nothing stirring in the house
Save one wee hungry nibbling mouse,
   Then why so busy thou ?

Nay !   Start not at that sparkling light ;
'Tis but the moon that shines so bright
On the window pane bedropped with rain :
Then little Darling ! Sleep again,
   And wake when it is day.
D. Wordsworth

17. A Sleeping Child

   Lips, lips ! open !
Up comes a little bird that lives inside,
Up comes a little bird, and peeps, and out he
   flies.

All the day he sits inside, and sometimes he
   sings ;

Up he comes and out he goes at night to spread
  his wings.

Little bird, little bird, whither will you go ?
Round about the world while nobody can
  know.

Little bird, little bird, whither do you flee ?
Far away round the world while nobody can
  see.

Little bird, little bird, how long will you roam ?
All round the world, and around again home,

Round the round world, and back through the
  air ;
When the morning comes, the little bird is
  there.

Back comes the little bird, and looks, and in
  he flies,
Up awakes the little boy, and opens both his
  eyes.

Sleep, sleep, little boy, little bird's away,
Little bird will come again by the peep of day.

Sleep, sleep, little boy, little bird must go
Round about the world, while nobody can
  know.

Sleep, sleep sound, little bird goes round,
Round and round he goes—sleep, sleep sound !
A. H. CLOUGH

18. BED-TIME

THE evening is coming,
The sun sinks to rest,
The rooks are all flying
Straight home to the nest.
' Caw ! " says the rook, as he flies overhead,
" It's time little people were going to bed ! "

The flowers are closing :
The daisy's asleep,
The primrose is buried
In slumber so deep.
Shut up for the night is the pimpernel red ;
It's time little people were going to bed !

The butterfly, drowsy,
Has folded its wing ;
The bees are returning
No more the birds sing.
Their labour is over, their nestlings are fed ;
It's time little people were going to bed !

Here comes the pony,
His work is all done,

B

Down through the meadow
He takes a good run.
Up go his heels, and down goes his head,
It's time little people were going to bed.

Good-night, little people,
Good-night and good-night :
Sweet dreams to your eyelids
Till dawning of light ;
The evening has come, there's no more to be
said :
It's time little people were going to bed !

T. HOOD

19. THE LAND OF STORY BOOKS

At evening when the lamp is lit,
Around the fire my parents sit,
They sit at home and talk and sing,
And do not play at anything.

Now, with my little gun I crawl
All in the dark along the wall,
And follow round the forest track
Away behind the sofa back.

There, in the night, where none can spy,
All in my hunter's camp I lie,
And play at books that I have read
Till it is time to go to bed.

These are the hills, these are the woods,
These are my starry solitudes ;
And there the river by whose brink
The roaring lions come to drink.

I see the others far away,
As if in firelit camp they lay,
And I, like to an Indian scout,
Around their party prowled about.

So, when my nurse comes in for me,
Home I return across the sea,
And go to bed with backward looks
At my dear land of story books.

R. L. STEVENSON

20. BABYLAND

"How many miles to Babyland ? "
   "Any one can tell !
   Up one flight ;
   To the right.
Please to ring the bell."

"What can you see in Babyland ? "
   "Little folks in white—
   Downy heads,
   Cradle-beds,
Faces pure and bright."

"What do they do in Babyland?"
    "Dream, and wake, and play
    Laugh and crow,
    Shout and grow.
Jolly times have they!"

"What do they say in Babyland?"
    "Why, the oddest things!
    Might as well
    Try to tell
What a birdie sings!"

"Who is the Queen of Babyland?"
    "Mother, kind and sweet;
    And her love,
    Born above,
Guides the little feet."

GEORGE COOPER

21. WISHING

RING—TING! I wish I were a Primrose,
A bright yellow Primrose blowing in the
        Spring!
    The stooping boughs above me,
    The wandering bee to love me,
    The fern and moss to keep across,
        And the Elm-tree for our King!

Nay—stay! I wish I were an Elm-tree,
A great lofty Elm-tree, with green leaves gay!

The winds would set them dancing,
The sun and moonshine glancing,
The Birds would house among the boughs,
And sweetly sing !

O—no ! I wish I were a Robin,
A Robin or a little Wren, everywhere to go ;
Through forest, field, or garden,
And ask no leave or pardon.
Till Winter comes with icy thumbs
To ruffle up our wing.

Well—tell ! Where should I fly to,
Where go to sleep in the dark wood or dell ?
Before a day was over,
Home comes the rover,
For Mother's kiss—sweeter this
Than any other thing !

W. ALLINGHAM

22. THE PEDLAR'S CARAVAN

I WISH I lived in a caravan,
With a horse to drive like a pedlar-man !
Where he comes from nobody knows,
Or where he goes to ; but on he goes !

His caravan has windows two,
And a chimney of tin, that the smoke comes
through,

He has a wife, with a baby brown,
And they go riding from town to town.

Chairs to mend, and delf[1] to sell !
He clashes the basins like a bell :
Tea-trays, baskets ranged in order,
Plates with the alphabet round the border !

The roads are brown, and the sea is green,
But his house is just like a bathing-machine ;
The world is round, and he can ride,
Rumble and splash, to the other side !

With the pedlar-man I should like to roam,
And write a book when I came home ;
All the people would read my book,
Just like the Travels of Captain Cook ![2]

W. B. RANDS

23. A LOBSTER QUADRILLE

" WILL you walk a little faster ?" said a whiting
      to a snail,
" There's a porpoise close behind us, and he's
      treading on my tail.

[1] *Delf.* Glazed earthenware pottery, so called because it was originally made in the town of Delft, or Delf, in Holland.

[2] Captain Cook was the first man who sailed round the world, 1768-1771.

See how eagerly the lobsters and the turtles
    all advance !
They are waiting on the shingle—will you
    come and join the dance ?
Will you, won't you, will you, won't you, will
    you join the dance ?
Will you, won't you, will you, won't you,
    won't you join the dance ?

" You can have no notion how delightful it
    will be
When they take us up and throw us, with
    the lobsters, out to sea ! "
But the snail replied, " Too far, too far ! "
    and gave a look askance—
Said he thanked the whiting kindly, but he
    would not join the dance,
Would not, could not, would not, could not,
    would not join the dance.
Would not, could not, would not, could not,
    could not join the dance.

" What matters it how far we go ? " his scaly
    friend replied.
"There is another shore, you know, upon the
    other side.
The further off from England the nearer is
    to France—
Then turn not pale, beloved snail, but come
    and join the dance,

Will you, won't you, will you, won't you, will
    you join the dance ?
Will you, won't you, will you, won't you,
    won't you join the dance ? "

LEWIS CARROLL

24. THE CHERRY TREE

UP into a cherry tree,
Who should climb but little me ?
I held the trunk with both my hands
And looked abroad on foreign lands.

I saw the next-door garden lie,
Adorned with flowers before my eye,
And many pleasant places more,
That I had never seen before.

I saw the dimpling river pass
And be the sky's blue looking-glass :
The dusty roads go up and down
With people trampling into town.

If I could find a higher tree,
Farther and farther I could see—
To where the grown-up river slips
Into the sea among the ships.

To where the roads on either hand
Lead onward into fairyland—
Where all the children dine at five
And all the playthings come alive.

R. L. Stevenson

25. Seven times One

" There's no dew left on the daisies and
　　clover ;
There's no rain left in heaven ;
I've said my seven times over and over,
' Seven times one are seven.' "

I am old, so old, I can write a letter,
My birthday lessons are done ;
The lambs play always, they know no better—
They're only once time one.

Oh ! moon in the night, I have seen you
　　smiling,
And shining so round and low ;
You were bright ! Ah bright, but your light
　　is failing,
You're nothing now but a bow.

You moon, have you done something wrong
　　in heaven,
That God has hidden your face ?

I hope, if you have, you may soon be forgiven,
And shine again in your place.

Oh ! velvet bee you're a dusty fellow,
You've powdered your legs with gold :
Oh ! brave marsh marybuds,[1] rich and yellow,
Give me your money to hold.

Oh ! columbine open your golden wrapper,
Where two twin turtle-doves dwell :
Oh ! cuckoo-pint toll me your purple clapper,
That hangs in your clear green bell.

And show me your nest with the young ones
    in it,
I will not steal them away ;
I am old, you may trust me, linnet, linnet,
I'm seven times one to-day.

J. INGELOW

26. VALENTINE'S DAY[2]

OH ! I wish I were a tiny browny bird from
    out the south,
Settled among the alder-holts,[3] and twittering
    by the stream ;

[1] *Marybuds.* Marigolds.

[2] St Valentine's Day is the 14th of February ; early in the spring the birds choose their mates for the summer.

[3] *Alder-holts.* Small woods of alders, which generally grow in moist places.

I would put my tiny tail down, and put up
  my tiny mouth,
And sing my tiny life away in one melodious
  dream.
I would sing about the blossoms, and the
  sunshine and the sky,
And the tiny wife I mean to have in such a
  cosy nest ;
And if some one came and shot me dead, why
  then I could but die,
With my tiny life and tiny song just ended at
  their best.

C. KINGSLEY

27. THE FAIRIES

Up the airy mountain,
Down the rushy glen,
We daren't go a-hunting,
For fear of little men ;
Wee folk, good folk,
Trooping all together ;
Green jacket, red cap,
And white owl's feather !

Down along the rocky shore
Some make their home,
They live on crispy pancakes
Of yellow tide-foam ;

Some in the reeds
Of the black mountain-lake,
With frogs for their watch-dogs,
All night awake.
High on the hill-top
The old King sits ;
He is now so old and gray
He's nigh lost his wits.
With a bridge of white mist
Columbkill he crosses,
On his stately journeys
From Slieveleague to Rosses :
Or going up with music
On cold starry nights,
To sup with the Queen
Of the gay Northern Lights.

They stole little Bridget
For seven years long ;
When she came down again,
Her friends were all gone.
They took her lightly back,
Between the night and morrow,
They thought that she was fast asleep,
But she was dead with sorrow.
They have kept her ever since
Deep within the lake,
On a bed of flag-leaves,
Watching till she wake.

By the craggy hill-side,
Through the mosses bare
They have planted thorn-trees,
For pleasure here and there.
Is any man so daring
As dig them up in spite,
He shall find their sharpest thorns
In his bed at night.

Up the airy mountain,
Down the rushy glen,
We daren't go a-hunting,
For fear of little men ;
Wee folk, good folk,
Trooping all together ;
Green jacket, red cap,
And white owl's feather !

W. ALLINGHAM

28. MY TREASURES

THESE nuts, that I keep in the back of the nest
Where all my lead soldiers are lying at rest,
Were gathered in autumn by nursie and me
In a wood with a well by the side of the sea.

This whistle was made (and how clearly it
      sounds !)
By the side of a field at the end of the grounds.
Of a branch of a plane, with a knife of my own—
It was nursie who made it, and nursie alone !

The stone, with the white and the yellow and
    grey,
We discovered I cannot tell *how* far away ;
And I carried it back although weary and cold,
For though father denies it, I'm sure it is
    gold.

But of all my treasures the last is the king,
For there's very few children possess such a
    thing ;
And that is a chisel, both handle and blade,
Which a man who was really a carpenter
    made.

R. L. STEVENSON

PART II

1. A Charm

In the morning when you rise
Wash your hands and cleanse your eyes,
Next, be sure ye have a care
To disperse the water far:
For as far as it doth light,
So far keeps the evil sprite.

R. Herrick

2. A Riddle—(a Tree)

I have only one foot, but thousands of toes;
My one foot stands well, but never goes;
I've a good many arms, if you count them all,
But hundreds of fingers, large and small;
From the ends of my fingers my beauty
grows;
I breathe with my hair, and I drink with my
toes;
I grow bigger and bigger about the waist
Although I am always very tight laced;

None e'er saw me eat—I've no mouth to bite !
Yet I eat all day, and digest all night.
In the summer with song I shake and quiver
But in winter I fast and groan and shiver.

G. MACDONALD

3. CURFEW

SOLEMNLY, mournfully,
  Dealing its dole,
The Curfew Bell,
  Is beginning to toll.

Cover the embers,
  And put out the light ;
Toil comes with the morning,
  And rest with the night.

Dark grow the windows,
  And quenched is the fire.
Sound fades into silence,—
  All footsteps retire.

No voice in the chambers,
  No sound in the hall !
Sleep and oblivion
  Reign over all.

H. W. LONGFELLOW

4. The Moon

LADY MOON, Lady Moon, where are you
    roving ?
      Over the sea.
Lady Moon, Lady Moon, whom are you
    loving ?
      All that love me.

Are you not tired with rolling, and never
      Resting to sleep ?
Why look so pale, and so sad, as for ever
      Wishing to weep ?

Ask me not this, little child ! If you love me ;
      You are too bold ;
I must obey my dear Father above me,
      And do as I'm told.

Lady Moon, Lady Moon, where are you
    roving ?
      Over the sea.
Lady Moon, Lady Moon, whom are you
    loving ?
      All that love me

          LORD HOUGHTON

C

5. THE LAMB

Little Lamb, who made thee ?
Dost thou know who made thee ?
Gave thee life, and bid thee feed,
By the stream and o'er the mead ;
  Gave thee clothing of delight,
  Softest clothing, woolly, bright ;
Gave thee such a tender voice,
Making all the vales rejoice ?
  Little Lamb, who made thee ?
  Dost thou know who made thee ?

Little Lamb, I'll tell thee,
Little Lamb, I'll tell thee :
He is callèd by thy name,
For He calls Himself a Lamb.
  He is meek, and He is mild :
  He became a little child.
I, a child, and thou a Lamb,
We are callèd by His name.
  Little Lamb, God bless thee !
  Little Lamb, God bless thee !

W. BLAKE

6. THE WORLD

Great, wide, beautiful, wonderful world,
With the wonderful water round you curled,

And the wonderful grass upon your breast—
World, you are beautifully drest.

The wonderful air is over me,
And the wonderful wind is shaking the tree,
It walks on the water and whirls the mills,
And talks to itself on the tops of the hills.

You friendly Earth ! How far you go,
With the wheat-fields that nod, and the rivers
    that flow,
With cities and gardens, and cliffs and isles,
And people upon you for thousands of miles ?

Ah ! You are so great, and I am so small,
I tremble to think of you, World, at all ;
And yet when I said my prayers to-day,
A whisper inside me seemed to say,
" You are more than the Earth, though you
    are such a dot ;
You can love and think, and the Earth can
    not ! "

                      W. B. RANDS

7. THE DAISY'S SONG

THE sun, with his great eye,
Sees not so much as I ;
And the moon, all silver, proud,
Might as well be in a cloud.

And O the spring—the spring !
I lead the life of a king !
Couch'd in the teeming[1] grass,
I spy each pretty lass.

I look where no one dares,
And I stare where no one stares,
And, when the night is nigh,
Lambs bleat my lullaby.

J. KEATS

8. LITTLE GARAINE

[There are two constellations or groups of stars in the
heavens called "The Great Bear" and "The Little Bear."
The mountains and valleys on the moon's surface assume
from the earth the appearance of a man, carrying a bundle
of sticks ; hence the expression, "The Man in the Moon."
In the broad circle in the heavens, called the Zodiac, are
the twelve signs through which the sun passes in its
annual course.]

" WHERE do the stars grow, little Garaine ?
The garden of moons, is it far away ?
The orchard of suns, my little Garaine,
Will you take us there some day ? "

' If you shut your eyes," quoth little Garaine,
I will show you the way to go

[1] *Teeming.* Plentiful, thick.

To the orchard of suns and the garden of
    moons
And the field where the stars do grow.

" But you must speak soft," quoth little
    Garaine,
" And still must your footsteps be,
For a great bear prowls in the field of stars,
And the moons they have men to see.

" And the suns have the children of Signs to
    guard,
And they know no pity at all—
You must not stumble, you must not speak,
When you come to the orchard wall.

" The gates are locked," quoth little Garaine,
" But the way I am going to tell!
The key of your heart it will open them all,
And there's where the darlings dwell!"

Sir Gilbert Parker

9. Written in March

The cock is crowing,
The stream is flowing,
The small birds twitter,
The lake doth glitter,
The green field sleeps in the sun;

The oldest and youngest
Are at work with the strongest :
The cattle are grazing,
Their heads never raising,
There are forty feeding like one !

Like an army defeated,
The snow hath retreated,
And now doth fare ill,
On the top of the bare hill ;
The ploughboy is whooping—anon—anon.
There's joy in the mountains,
There's life in the fountains ;
Small clouds are sailing,
Blue sky prevailing,
The rain is over and gone !

W. WORDSWORTH

10. BUTTERCUPS AND DAISIES

BUTTERCUPS and daisies,
Oh, the pretty flowers ;
Coming ere the spring time,
To tell of sunny hours.
While the trees are leafless,
While the fields are bare,
Buttercups and daisies
Spring up here and there

Ere the snow-drop peepeth,
Ere the crocus bold,
Ere the early primrose
Opes its paly gold,—
Somewhere on the sunny bank
Buttercups are bright;
Somewhere 'mong the frozen grass
Peeps the daisy white.

Little hardy flowers,
Like to children poor,
Playing in their sturdy health
By their mother's door.
Purple with the north-wind,
Yet alert and bold;
Fearing not, and caring not,
Though they be a-cold!

What to them is winter!
What are stormy showers!
Buttercups and daisies
Are these human flowers!
He, who gave them hardships
And a life of care,
Gave them likewise hardy strength
And patient hearts to bear.

M. Howitt

11. To a Bee

Thou wert out betimes, thou busy, busy bee !
As abroad I took my early way,
Before the cow from her resting-place
Had risen up, and left her trace
On the meadow, with dew so gay,
Saw I thee, thou busy, busy bee !

Thou wert working late, thou busy, busy bee !
After the fall of the cistus flower,[1]
When the primrose of evening was ready to
    burst,
I heard thee last, as I saw thee first ;
In the silence of the evening hour,
Heard I thee, thou busy, busy bee !

Thou art a miser, thou busy, busy bee !
Late and early at employ ;
Still on thy golden stores intent,
Thy summer in keeping and hoarding is
    spent,
What thy winter will never enjoy,
Wise lesson this for me, thou busy, busy bee !

Little dost thou think, thou busy, busy bee !
What is the end of thy toil,
When the latest flowers of the ivy are gone.

---

[1] *Cistus flower.* The rock-rose.

And all thy work for the year is done,
Thy master comes for the spoil ;
Woe then for thee, thou busy, busy bee !
R. Southey

12. The Lady-Bird

Lady-Bird ! Lady-bird ! Fly away home,
The field-mouse is gone to her nest,
The daisies have shut up their sleepy red eyes,
And the bees and the birds are at rest.

Lady-bird ! Lady-bird ! Fly away home,
The glow-worm is lighting her lamp,
The dew's falling fast, and your fine speckled
    wings
Will flag with the close-clinging damp.

Lady-bird ! Lady-bird ! Fly away home,
The fairy-bells tinkle afar ;
Make haste, or they'll catch you and harness
    you fast,
With a cobweb to Oberon's[1] car.
Mrs Montgomery

[1] *Oberon.* The king of the Fairies.

13. Song from *The Water Babies*

I ONCE had a sweet little doll, dears,
The prettiest doll in the world ;
Her cheeks were so red and so white, dears,
And her hair was so charmingly curled.
But I lost my poor little doll, dears,
As I played in the heath one day ;
And I cried for her more than a week, dears,
But I never could find where she lay.

I found my poor little doll, dears,
As I played in the heath one day ;
Folks say she is terribly changed, dears,
For her paint is all washed away.
And her arms trodden off by the cows, dears,
And her hair not the least bit curled ;
Yet for old sakes' sake she is still, dears,
The prettiest doll in the world.

C. KINGSLEY

14. The Blackbird

O BLACKBIRD ! sing me something well :
While all the neighbours shoot thee round,
I keep smooth plats of fruitful ground,
Where thou may'st warble, eat and dwell.

The espaliers and the standards all
Are thine ; the range of lawn and park :

The unnetted black-hearts ripen dark,
All thine, against the garden wall.

Yet in the sultry garden-squares,
Now thy flute-notes are changed to coarse,
I hear thee not at all, or hoarse
As when a hawker hawks his wares.

Take warning! he that will not sing
While yon sun prospers in the blue,
Shall sing for want, 'ere leaves are new,
Caught in the frozen palms of Spring.

LORD TENNYSON

15. THE OWL. (*Song*)

WHEN cats run home and light is come,
    And dew is cold upon the ground,
And the far-off stream is dumb,
    And the whirring sail goes round,
    And the whirring sail goes round,
        Alone and warming his five wits,
        The white owl in the belfry sits.

When merry milkmaids click the latch,
    And rarely smells the new-mown hay,
And the cock hath sung beneath the thatch,

Twice or thrice his roundelay,[1]
Twice or thrice his roundelay,
 Alone and warming his five wits,
 The white owl in the belfry sits.
      Lord Tennyson

16. The Land of Dreams

Awake, awake, my little boy !
Thou wast thy mother's only joy ;
Why dost thou weep in thy gentle sleep ?
Awake ! Thy father does thee keep.

" O, what land is the Land of Dreams ?
What are its mountains, and what are its
  streams ?
O father ! I saw my mother there,
Among the lilies by waters fair.

" Among the lambs, clothèd in white,
She walk'd with her Thomas in sweet delight ;
I wept for joy, like a dove I mourn,
O ! when shall I again return ? "

Dear child, I also by pleasant streams
Have wander'd all night in the Land of Dreams,
But tho' calm and warm the waters wide,
I could not get to the other side.

[1] *Roundelay.* A poem or song in which a phrase or
refrain is constantly repeated.

" Father, O father !   What do we here
In this land of unbelief and fear ?
The Land of Dreams is better far,
Above the light of the morning star."

W. BLAKE

17. ON SATURDAY MORNING EARLY

ON Saturday next at half-past eight—
I mustn't be half a second late—
I'm going out at the garden gate
    When the dew is glittery-pearly ;
I'm going, I'm going, I don't know where,
But I think I shall find some others there,
On Saturday next if the sun shines fair,
    On Saturday morning early.

Perhaps it's the home of the big tom-tit,
Or the land where the little blue fairies flit,
For Daddy he said I should visit it,
    And go for a treat alone, too,
In a marvellous carriage with golden springs,
And six white horses with twelve white wings,
And a coachman all over curls and things,
    And a footman all of my own, too.

Or perhaps I shall go to the doll-country,
Where the dollies are all as big as me,

And all have raspberry jam for tea,
    With huge thick slices of *some* cake ;
It might be sponge, or it might be bright
With cherries, and iced as smooth and white,
As the pond when the feathery snow falls
    light,
    Or it might be, possibly, plum-cake.

What fun it'll be to see Boy Blue,
And Jack and the Stalk that grew and grew,
And Puss in Boots and his Marquis, too,
    And giants and giantesses ;
And wonderful gleaming golden towns,
And Kings with sceptres and swords and
    crowns,
And Queens with fur on their satin-gowns,
    And beautiful young princesses !

And if I should see Red Riding Hood,
And her grandmamma in the dark old wood,
I shall run away, as a good girl should
    For fear that a wolf might meet her.
But grandmamma will, perhaps, explain
If teeth, when they bite you, give you pain,
And how she ever got out again
    When the wolf had managed to eat her

And, oh, I shall find where the tulips go,
And the golden crocuses all aglow,
And where the little white daisies grow,

When they vanish away together ;
And the place where the pretty blue-bells stay,
And the pinks and the roses bright and gay,
When they go away and " Good-bye," they
     say,
  " Good-bye, for the winter weather."

I must take my funny dog Buff, the Skye,
With his little short legs, and his ears cocked
     high,
And his long rough hair, and his hidden eye,
  And his face like a great grey pansy.
Doll Jane I shall leave on the nursery floor,
For she doesn't go travelling any more :—
Since her head got squeezed in the bedroom
     door
  There's not very much she can see.

So I'm ready, I'm ready !   I've packed some
     socks,
A bonnet, a bib, and two holland frocks,
And a pair of shoes in a brand-new box ;
  And I've given my Mummy warning.
I shall take a mug and a fork and spoon,
And the musical box that plays one tune,
And I'll hurry away—but I'll come back
     soon—
  On Saturday next in the morning.
               R. C. LEHMANN

18. Song

April, April,
Laugh thy girlish laughter;
Then, the moment after,
Weep thy girlish tears!
April, that mine ears
Like a lover greetest,
If I tell thee, sweetest,
All my hopes and fears,
April, April,
Laugh thy golden laughter,
But, the moment after,
Weep thy golden tears!

W Watson

19. The Witches' Steeds

There are four wild steeds that the witches ride
Down the starry meadows shining and wide,
You can hear them snort as they gallop
    through,
Tugging their bridles of roped pearl-dew.
But never a one can be seen by you!

One is the North Wind; grey the sky
When he bites at the beeches, cantering by.
Hark to his madcap rider rate,
As she plucks at his forehead: " Straight!
    Go straight! "

One is the East Wind ; four elf-grooms
Fed him all day with the first spring blooms ;
But the country lasses, a-tired o' their Maying,
Hear him, still starved, in the night-time
neighing.

The West Wind, mad with his witch's spur,
Plunges and leaps, but he can't throw her !
And the children turn in their sleep and
wonder
When they hear his hoofs on the house-top
thunder.

The South Wind last ; behind him the leaves,
And the swallows come home to our English
eaves,
Oh ! He lifts each hoof so light and so light
That there's never a flower in the still, warm
night
That is crushed by the whinnying South
Wind's flight.

W. H. OGILVIE

20. DAFFY-DOWN-DILLY

DAFFY-DOWN-DILLY
Came up in the cold,
Through the brown mould,
Although the March breezes

D

Blew keen on her face,
Although the white snow
Lay on many a place.

Daffy-Down-Dilly
Had heard under ground,
The sweet rushing sound
Of the streams, as they broke
From their white winter chains,
Of the whistling spring winds
And the pattering rains.

" Now then," thought Daffy,
Deep down in her heart,
" It's time I should start."
So she pushed her soft leaves
Through the hard frozen ground,
Quite up to the surface
And then she looked round.

There was snow all about her,
Grey clouds overhead ;
The trees all looked dead ;
Then how do you think
Poor Daffy-down felt,
When the sun would not shine,
And the ice would not melt ?

" Cold weather ! " thought Daffy,
Still working away :

" The earth's hard to-day !
There's but half an inch
Of my leaves to be seen,
And two-thirds of that
Is more yellow than green.

" I can't do much yet ;
But I'll do what I can :
It's well I began !
For, unless I can manage
To lift up my head,
The people will think
That the Spring herself's dead."

So, little by little,
She brought her leaves out,
All clustered about ;
And then her bright flowers
Began to unfold,
Till Daffy stood robed
In her spring green and gold.

A. B. WARNER

21. HEIGHO, MY DEARIE

A MOONBEAM floateth from the skies,
Whispering : " Heigho, my dearie ;
I would spin a web before your eyes—
A beautiful web of silver light

Wherein is many a wondrous sight
Of a radiant garden leagues away,
Where the softly tinkling lilies sway
And the snow-white lambkins are at play—
Heigho, my dearie ! "

A brownie stealeth from the vine,
Singing : " Heigho, my dearie ;
And will you hear this song of mine—
A song of the land of murk and mist
Where bideth the bud the dew hath kist ?
Then let the moonbeam's web of light
Be spun before thee, silvery white,
And I shall sing the livelong night—
Heigho, my dearie ! "

The night wind speedeth from the sea,
Murmuring : " Heigho, my dearie ;
I bring a mariner's prayer for thee ;
So let the moonbeam veil thine eyes,
And the brownie sing thee lullabies—
But I shall rock thee to and fro,
Kissing the brow he loveth so,
And the prayer shall guard thy bed, I trow—
Heigho, my dearie ! "

EUGENE FIELD

22. Three Men of Gotham

" Seamen three !   What men be ye ? "
—" Gotham's three wise men we be."
—" Whither in your bowl so free ? "
—" To rake the moon from out the sea.
  The bowl goes trim.   The moon doth shine.
  And our ballast is old wine.—
—And your ballast is old wine."

" Who art thou, so fast adrift ? "
—" I am he, they call Old Care."
 —" Here on board we will thee lift."—
 —" No : I may not enter there."
—" Wherefore so ? "—" 'Tis Jove's decree,
  In a bowl Care may not be,
  In a bowl Care may not be."

—" Fear ye not the waves that roll ? "
—" No : in charmèd bowl we swim."
—" What the charm that floats the bowl ? "
—" Water may not pass the brim.
  The bowl goes trim.   The moon doth shine
  And our ballast is old wine.—
—And your ballast is old wine."

                                    T. L. Peacock

23. March

MARCH ! March ! They are coming
In troops to the tune of the wind :
Red-headed woodpeckers drumming,
Gold-crested thrushes behind ;
Sparrows in brown jackets hopping
Past every gateway and door ;
Finches with crimson caps stopping
Just where they stopped years before.

March ! March ! They are slipping
Into their places at last :
Little white lily-buds, dripping
Under the showers that fall fast ;
Buttercups, violets, roses ;
Snowdrop and bluebell and pink ;
Throng upon throng of sweet posies,
Bending the dewdrops to drink.

March ! March ! They will hurry
Forth at the wild bugle-sound ;
Blossoms and birds in a flurry,
Fluttering all over the ground.
Hang out your flags, birch and willow !
Shake out your red tassels, larch !
Up, blades of grass, from your pillow !
Hear who is calling you—March !

L. LARCOM

24. Hie Away

Hie away, hie away !
Over bank and over brae,
Where the copsewood is the greenest,
Where the fountains glisten sheenest,
Where the lady ferns grow strongest,
Where the morning dew lies longest,
Where the blackcock sweetest sips it,
Where the fairy latest trips it :
Hie to haunts right seldom seen,
Lovely, lonesome, cool, and green ;
Over bank and over brae,
Hie away, hie away.

Sir W. Scott

25. The Water ! The Water !

The Water !   The Water !
The joyous brook for me,
That tuneth through the quiet night
Its ever-living glee.
The Water !   The Water !
That sleepless, merry heart,
Which gurgles on unstintedly,
And loveth to impart
To all around it, some small measure
Of its own most perfect pleasure.

The Water !   The Water !
The gentle stream for me
That gushes from the old grey stone
Beside the alder tree.
The Water !   The Water !
That ever-bubbling spring
I loved and look'd on while a child,
In deepest wondering—
And ask'd it whence it came and went,
And when its treasures would be spent.

The Water !   The Water !
The merry wanton brook
That bent itself to pleasure me,
Like mine old shepherd crook.
The Water !   The Water !
That sang so sweet at noon,
And sweeter still all night, to win
Smiles from the pale, proud moon,
And from the little fairy faces
That gleam in heaven's remotest places.

W. MOTHERWELL

26. THE RIVULET

RUN, little rivulet, run !
Summer is fairly begun.
Bear to the meadow the hymn of the pines,
And the echo that rings where the waterfall
shines ;
Run, little rivulet, run !

Run, little rivulet, run !
Sing to the fields of the sun,
That wavers in emerald, shivers in gold,
Where you glide from your rocky ravine
    crystal-cold ;
Run, little rivulet, run !

Run, little rivulet, run !
Sing of the flowers, every one,—
Of the delicate harebell and violet blue ;
Of the red mountain-rosebud, all dripping
    with dew ;
Run, little rivulet, run !

Run, little rivulet, run !
Carry the perfume you won
From the lily that woke when the morning
    was grey
To the white waiting moonbeam adrift on the
    bay :
Run, little rivulet, run !

Run, little rivulet, run !
Stay not till summer is done !
Carry the city the mountain-birds' glee ;
Carry the joy of the hills to the sea ;
Run, little rivulet, run !

L. LARCOM

27. THE ANT OR EMMET

THESE Emmets, how little they are in our
    eyes !
We tread them to dust and a troop of them
    dies,
      Without our regard or concern ;
Yet as wise as we are, if we went to their
    school,
There's many a sluggard, and many a fool,
      Some lessons of wisdom might learn.

They don't wear their time out in sleeping or
    play,
But gather up corn in a sun-shiny day,
      And for winter they lay up their store :
They manage their work in such regular
    forms,
One would think they foresaw all the frost
    and the storms,
      And so brought their food within doors.

But I have less sense than a poor creeping ant,
If I take not due care for the things I shall
    want,
      Nor provide against dangers in time.
When death or old age shall stare in my face,
What a wretch shall I be at the end of my days,
      If I trifle away all their prime.

Now, now, while my strength and my youth
    are in bloom
Let me think what will serve me when sickness
    shall come,
      And pray that my sins be forgiven ;
Let me read in good books and believe and
    obey,
That when death turns me out of this cottage
    of clay,
      I may dwell in a palace in heaven.

                    I. WATTS

28. LITTLE SHIPS IN THE AIR

" FLAKES of snow with sails so white,
    Drifting down the wintry skies,
Tell me where your route begins,
    Say which way your harbour lies."

" In the clouds, the roomy clouds,
    Arching earth with shadowy dome,
There's the port from which we sail,
    There is tiny snow-flake's home."

" And the cargo that you take
    From these cloudy ports above,—
Is it always meant to bless,
    Sent in anger or in love ? "

" Warmth for all the tender roots,
    Warmth for every living thing,
Water for the river's flow,
    This the cargo that we bring."

" Who's the master that you serve,
    Bids you lift your tiny sails,
Brings you safely to the earth,
    Guides you through the wintry gales ? "

" He who tells the birds to sing,
    He who sends the April flowers,
He who ripens all our fruit,
    That great Master, He is ours."

                                    E. A. RAND

29. THE FLOWERS

WHEN love arose in heart and deed
To wake the world to greater joy,
" What can she give me now ? " said Greed,
Who thought to win some costly toy.

He rose, he ran, he stoop'd, he clutch'd ;
And soon the Flowers that Love let fall,
In Greed's hot grasp were fray'd and
    smutch'd,
And Greed said, " Flowers ! Can this be all ? "

He flung them down and went his way.
He cared no jot for thyme or rose,
But boys and girls came out to play,
And some took these and some took those—

Red, blue, and white, and green and gold ;
And at their touch the dew return'd,
And all the bloom a thousandfold—
So red, so ripe, the roses burn'd !

W. B. RANDS

30. ANSWER TO A CHILD'S QUESTION

Do you ask what the birds say ? The
  sparrow and the dove,
The linnet, and thrush say, " I love, and I
  love ! "
In the winter they're silent, the wind is so
  strong :
What it says I don't know, but it sings a loud
  song.
But green leaves, and blossoms, and sunny
  warm weather,
And singing and loving—all come back
  together.
But the lark is so brimful of gladness and love,
The green fields below him, the blue sky above.
That he sings, and he sings, and forever sings he,
" I love my Love, and my Love loves me."

S. T. COLERIDGE

31. Over the Hills and Far Away

Over the hills and far away,
A little boy steals from his morning play,
And under the blossoming apple-tree
He lies and he dreams of the things to be :
Of battles fought and of victories won,
Of wrongs o'erthrown and of great deeds done—
Of the valour that he shall prove some day,
Over the hills and far away.
Over the hills and far away !

Over the hills and far away,
It's, oh, for the toil the livelong day !
But it mattereth not to the soul aflame
With a love for riches and power and fame !
On, O man ! while the sun is high—
On to the certain joys that lie
Yonder where blazeth the noon of day,
Over the hills and far away—
Over the hills and far away !

Over the hills and far away,
An old man lingers at close of day ;
Now that his journey is almost done,
His battles fought and his victories won—
The old-time honesty and truth,
The trustfulness and the friends of youth,
Home and mother—where are they ?

Over the hills and far away—
Over the years and far away !

EUGENE FIELD

32. WHAT WAY DOES THE WIND COME ?

[This poem was written for Wordsworth's little son
Edward, generally called " Johnnie " at home.]

WHAT way does the wind come ?   What way
    does he go ?
He rides over the water and over the snow,
Through wood and through vale ; and o'er
    rocky height,
Which the goat cannot climb, takes his
    sounding flight ;
He tosses about in every bare tree,
As, if you look up, you plainly may see ;
But how he will come, and whither he goes,
There's never a scholar in England knows.

He will suddenly stop in a cunning nook,
And ring a sharp 'larum ;—but, if you should
    look,
There's nothing to see but a cushion of snow,
Round as a pillow, and whiter than milk,
And softer than if it were covered with silk.
Sometimes he'll hide in the cave of a rock,

Then whistle as shrill as the buzzard cock ; [1]
—Yet seek him—and what shall you find in the
　　place ?
Nothing but silence and empty space ;
Save, in a corner, a heap of dry leaves,
That he's left, for a bed, to beggars or thieves !

As soon as 'tis daylight to-morrow, with me
You shall go to the orchard, and then you will
　　see
That he has been there, and made a great rout,
And cracked the branches, and strewn them
　　about ;
Heaven grant that he spare but that one
　　upright twig
That looked up at the sky so proud and big
All last summer, as well you know,
Studded with apples, a beautiful show !

Hark ! over the roof he makes a pause,
And growls as if he would fix his claws
Right in the slates, and with a huge rattle
Drive them down, like men in a battle ;
—But let him range round ; he does us no
　　harm,
We build up the fire, we're snug and warm ;
Untouched by his breath, see, the candle
　　shines bright,
And burns with a clear and steady light ;

[1] *Buzzard.* A greedy bird of the falcon family.

Books have we to read—but that half-stifled
  knell,
Alas ! 'tis the sound of the eight o'clock bell.

—Come now we'll to bed ! and when we are
  there
He may work his own will, and what shall we
  care ?
He may knock at the door,—we'll not let him
  in ;
May drive at the windows,—we'll laugh at his
  din ;
Let him seek his own home wherever it be ;
Here's a " cozie " warm house for Edward
  and me.

D. WORDSWORTH

33. A TRAGIC STORY

THERE lived a sage in days of yore,
And he a handsome pigtail wore ;
But wondered much, and sorrowed more,
Because it hung behind him.

He mused upon this curious case,
And swore he'd change the pigtail's place,
And have it hanging at his face,
Not dangling there behind him.

Says he, " The mystery I've found,—
I'll turn me round "—he turned him round ;
But still it hung behind him.

E

Then round and round, and out and in,
All day the puzzled sage did spin ;
In vain—it mattered not a pin—
The pigtail hung behind him.

And right and left, and round about,
And up and down and in and out
He turned ; but still the pigtail stout
Hung steadily behind him.

And though his efforts never slack,
And though he twist, and twirl, and tack,
Alas !   Still faithful to his back,
The pigtail hangs behind him.

W. M. THACKERAY

34. THE WIND AND THE MOON

SAID the Wind to the Moon, "I will blow you
    out !
                You stare
                In the air
                Like a ghost in the chair,
Always looking what I am about—
I hate to be watched ; I'll blow you out."

The Wind blew hard, and out went the Moon ;
                So deep
                On a heap
                Of cloudless sleep

Down lay the Wind, and slumbered soon,
Muttering low, " I've done for that Moon."

He turned in his bed ; she was there again !
        On high
        In the sky
        With her ghost eye,
The Moon shone white and alive and plain ;
Said the Wind, " I'll blow you out again."

He blew, and he blew, and the thread was gone,
        In the air
        Nowhere
        Was a moonbeam bare ;
Far off and silent the shy stars shone—
Sure and certain the Moon was gone !

The Wind he took to his revels once more ;
        On down
        In town
        Like a merry, mad clown,
He leaped and hallooed with whistle and roar ;
" What's that ? "—the glittering thread once
    more.

He flew in a rage—he danced and he blew ;
        But in vain
        Was the pain
        Of his bursting brain ;

For still broader the moon-scrap grew,
The broader he swelled his big cheeks and
    blew.

Slowly she grew—till she filled the night,
                    And shone
                    On her throne
                    In the sky alone,
A matchless, wonderful, silvery light,
Radiant and lovely, the queen of the night.

Said the Wind : " What a marvel of power
    am I ! "
                    With my breath
                    Good faith
                    I blew her to death—
First blew her away right out of the sky—
Then blew her in : what a strength am I ! "

But the Moon she knew nothing about the
    affair,
                    For high
                    In the sky,
                    With her one white eye
Motionless, miles above the air,
She had never heard the great Wind blare.[1]

                        G. MACDONALD

[1] *Blare.*   To make a loud noise like that of a trumpet.

35. THE WIND IN A FROLIC

THE wind one morning sprang up from sleep,
Saying, " Now for a frolic ! now for a leap !
Now for a mad-cap galloping chase !
I'll make a commotion in every place ! "

So it swept with a bustle right through a great
town,
Cracking the signs and scattering down
Shutters ; and whisking, with merciless
squalls,
Old women's bonnets and gingerbread stalls.
There never was heard a much lustier shout,
As the apples and oranges trundled about ;
And the urchins that stand with their thievish
eyes
For ever on watch, ran off each with a prize.

Then away to the field it went blustering and
humming,
And the cattle all wonder'd whatever was
coming ;
It pluck'd by the tails the grave matronly
cows,
And toss'd the colts' manes all over their
brows ;
Till, offended at such an unusual salute,
They all turn'd their backs, and stood sulky
and mute.

So on it went capering and playing its pranks,
Whistling with reeds on the broad river's
      banks,
Puffing the birds as they sat on the spray,
Or the traveller grave on the king's highway.

It was not too nice to hustle the bags
Of the beggar, and flutter his dirty rags ;
'Twas so bold, that it feared not to play its
      joke
With the doctor's wig or the gentleman's
      cloak,
Through the forest it roar'd, and cried gaily,
      " Now,
You sturdy old oaks, I'll make you bow ! "

And it made them bow without much ado,
Or it crack'd their great branches through and
      through.
Then it rushed like a monster on cottage and
      farm,
Striking their dwellings with sudden alarm ;
And they ran out like bees in a mid-summer
      swarm.
There were dames with their kerchiefs tied
      over their caps
To see if their poultry were free from mishaps ;

The turkeys they gobbled, the geese scream'd
      aloud,

And the hens crept to roost in a terrified
    crowd ;
There was rearing of ladders, and logs laying
    on,
Where the thatch from the roof threaten'd
    soon to be gone.
But the wind had swept on, and had met in a
    lane
With a schoolboy, who panted and struggled
    in vain ;
For it toss'd him, and twirl'd him, then pass'd,
    and he stood
With his hat in a pool, and his shoes in the
    mud.

Then away went the wind in its holiday glee,
And now it was far on the billowy sea,
And the lordly ships felt its staggering blow,
And the little boats darted to and fro !
But lo ! it was night, and it sank to rest
On the sea-bird's rock in the gleaming west,
Laughing to think, in its fearful fun,
How little of mischief it had done.

                        W. HOWITT

PART III

1. A Ceremony for Candlemas Day [1]

Down with the rosemary and so
Down with the bays and mistletoe ;
Down with the holly, ivy, all
Wherewith ye dressed the Christmas hall ;
That so the superstitious find
No one least branch there left behind ;
For look, how many leaves then be
Neglected there, maids, trust to me
So many goblins you shall see.

R. Herrick

2. The Year's at the Spring

The year's at the spring,
The day's at the morn ;
Morning's at seven ;
The hill-side's dew-pearled ;
The lark's on the wing ;
The snail's on the thorn :
God's in His heaven—
All's right with the world.

R. Browning

[1] *Candlemas Day.* February 2nd, the day set apart to commemorate the Purification of the Virgin Mary.

3. The Morning

Oh, come ! For the lily
  Is white on the lea,
Oh, come ! For the wood-doves
  Are paired on the tree ;
The lark sings, with dew
  On her wings and her feet ;
The thrush pours his ditty
  Loud, varied, and sweet ;
So come where the twin hares
  'Mid fragrance have been,
And with flowers I will weave thee
  A crown like a queen.

Oh, come ! Hark, the throstle
  Invites you aloud,
And wild comes the plover's cry
  Down from the cloud ;
The stream lifts its voice,
  And yon daisy's begun
To part its red lips
  And drink dew in the sun ;
The sky laughs in light,
  Earth rejoices in green ;
So come, and I'll crown thee
  With flowers like a queen.

Oh, haste ! Hark, the shepherd
  Hath wakened his pipe,

And led out his lambs
  Where the blackberry's ripe :
The bright sun is tasting
  The dew on the thyme,
Yon glad maiden's lilting [1]
  An old bridal rhyme,
There's joy in the heaven
  And gladness on earth—
So come to the sunshine
  And mix in the mirth.

A. CUNNINGHAM

4. THE FOUNTAIN

INTO the sunshine
Full of the light,
Leaping and flashing
From morn till night !

Into the moonlight,
Whiter than snow,
Waving so flower-like
When the winds blow !

Into the starlight
Rushing in spray,
Happy at midnight
Happy by day !

[1] *Lilting.*   Singing joyously.

Ever in motion,
Blithesome and cheery,
Still climbing heavenward,
Never aweary.

Glad of all weathers
Still seeming best,
Upward or downward
Motion thy rest.

Full of a nature
Nothing can tame,
Changed every moment,
Ever the same.

Ceaseless aspiring,
Ceaseless content,
Darkness or sunshine
Thy element.

Glorious fountain !
Let my heart be
Fresh, changeful, constant,
Upward like thee !

J. R. LOWELL

5. The Shepherd

How sweet is the shepherd's sweet lot !
  From the morn to the evening he strays ;
He shall follow his sheep all the day,
  And his tongue shall be fillèd with praise.

For he hears the lamb's innocent call,
  And he hears the ewe's tender reply ;
He is watchful while they are in peace,
  For they know when their shepherd is nigh.

W. Blake

6. The First Sight of Spring

The hazel-blooms, in threads of crimson hue,
Peep through the swelling buds, foretelling
    spring,
Ere yet a white-thorn leaf appears in view,
Or March finds throstles pleased enough to
    sing.
To the old touchwood-tree woodpeckers cling
A moment, and their harsh-toned notes renew ;
In happier mood, the stock-dove [1] claps his
    wing ;
The squirrel sputters up the powdered oak,
With tail cocked o'er his head, and ears erect,
Startled to hear the woodman's understroke ;

---

[1] *Stock-dove.* The wood-pigeon.

And with the courage which his fears collect,
He hisses fierce, half malice and half glee,
Leaping from branch to branch about the tree,
In winter's foliage, moss and lichens, deckt

J. CLARE

7. GREEN FIELDS OF ENGLAND

GREEN fields of England ! wheresoe'er
Across this watery waste we fare,
One image at our hearts we bear,
Green fields of England everywhere.

Sweet eyes in England, I must flee
Past where the waves' last confines be,
Ere your loved smile I cease to see,
Sweet eyes in England, dear to me !

Dear home in England, safe and fast
If but in thee my lot lie cast,
The past shall seem a nothing past
To thee, dear home, if won at last ;
Dear home in England, won at last.

A. H. CLOUGH

8. The Tree

The Tree's early leaf buds were bursting
    their brown ;
" Shall I take them away ? " said the Frost,
    sweeping down.
           " No, leave them alone
           Till the blossoms have grown,"
Prayed the Tree, while he trembled from
    rootlet to crown.

The Tree bore his blossoms, and all the birds
    sung :
" Shall I take them away ? " said the Wind,
    as he swung.
           " No, leave them alone
           Till the berries have grown,"
Said the Tree, while his leaflets quivering
    hung.

The Tree bore his fruit in the mid-summer
    glow :
Said the girl, " May I gather thy berries
    now ? "
           " Yes, all thou canst see :
           Take them, all are for thee,"
Said the Tree, while he bent down his laden
    boughs low.

B. Björnson

(From Björnson's Arne. *London, Heinemann.)*

9. MAY

MAY, thou month of rosy beauty,
Month when pleasure is a duty;
Month of bees, and month of flowers,
Month of blossom-laden bowers;
O thou merry month complete,
May, thy very name is sweet!
I no sooner write the word
Than it seems as though it heard,
And looks up, and laughs at me,
Like a sweet face, rosily;
Like an actual colour bright
Flushing from the paper's white.
If the rains that do us wrong
Come to keep the winter long,
And deny us thy sweet looks.
I can love thee, sweet in books;
Love thee in the poet's pages,
Where they keep thee green for ages;
May's in Milton, May's in Prior,
May's in Chaucer, Thomson, Dyer;
May's in all the Italian books;
She has old and modern nooks,
Where she sleeps with nymphs and elves
In happy places they call shelves,
With a drapery thick with blooms,
And will rise and dress your rooms.
Come, ye rains, then, if you will,
May's at home, and with me still;

But come rather thou, good weather,
And find us in the fields together.

LEIGH HUNT

10. IMPROMPTU

THE sun has long been set,
The stars are out by twos and threes,
The little birds are piping yet
Among the bushes and trees ;
There's a cuckoo, and one or two thrushes,
And a far-off wind that rushes,
And a sound of water that gushes,
And the cuckoo's sovereign cry
Fills all the hollow of the sky.
Who would go " parading "
In London, " and masquerading,"
On such a night of June,
With that beautiful soft half-moon,
And all these innocent blisses ?
On such a night as this is ?

W. WORDSWORTH

11. The Procession of the Flowers

First came the primrose,
On the bank, high,
Like a maiden looking forth
From the window of a tower
When the battle rolls below,
So look'd she,
And saw the storms go by.

Then came the wind-flower [1]
In the valley left behind,
As a wounded maiden, pale
With purple streaks of woe,
When the battle has roll'd by,
Wanders to and fro,
So totter'd she,
Dishevell'd in the wind.

Then came the daisies,
On the first of May,
Like a banner'd show's advance
While the crowd runs by the way,
With ten thousand flowers they came
Trooping through the fields.

As a happy people come,
So came they,
As a happy people come

[1] *Wind-flower.* The anemone.

F

When the war has roll'd away,
With dance and tabor, dance and drum,
And all make holiday.

Then came the cowslips,
Like a dancer in the fair,
She spread her little mat of green,
And on it danced she,
With a fillet [1] bound about her brow,
A golden fillet round her brow,
And rubies in her hair.

S. Dobell

12. The Housekeeper

The frugal snail, with forecast of repose,
Carries his house with him, where'er he goes ;
Peeps out—and if there comes a shower of
    rain,
Retreats to his small domicile amain.

Touch but a tip of him, a horn,—'tis well—
He curls up in his sanctuary shell.
He's his own landlord, his own tenant stay
Long as he will, he dreads no quarter day.
Himself he boards and lodges ; both invites
And feasts himself ; sleeps with himself
    o' nights.

[1] *Fillet.* A little band.

He spares the upholsterer trouble to procure
Chattels ; himself is his own furniture,
And his sole riches.   Wheresoe'er he roam—
Knock when you will,—he's sure to be at
    home.

C. Lamb

13. The Sea

The sea, the sea, the open sea,
The blue, the fresh, the ever free !
Without a mark, without a bound,
It runneth the earth's wide regions round ;
It plays with the clouds ; it mocks the skies
Or like a cradled creature lies.

I'm on the sea !   I'm on the sea !
I am where I would ever be ;
With the blue above, and the blue below,
And silence wheresoe'er I go ;
If a storm should come and awake the deep,
What matter ?   I shall ride and sleep.

I love—oh, how I love !—to ride
On the fierce, foaming, bursting tide,
When every mad wave drowns the moon
Or whistles aloft his tempest tune,
And tells how he goeth the world below,
And why the sou'west blasts do blow.

I never was on the dull, tame shore,
But I loved the great sea more and more,
And backward flew to her billowy breast,
Like a bird that seeketh its mother's nest ;
And a mother she was and is to me,
For I was born on the open sea.

The waves were white, and red the morn
In the noisy hour when I was born ;
And the whale it whistled, the porpoise rolled,
And the dolphins bared their backs of gold ;
And never was heard such an outcry wild
As welcomed to life the ocean-child !

I've lived since then, in calm and strife,
Full fifty summers a sailor's life ;
With wealth to spend and a power to range,
And never have sought nor sighed for change ;
And Death, whenever he comes to me,
Shall come on the wide, unbounded sea !

BARRY CORNWALL

14. UP, UP ! YE DAMES AND LASSES GAY !

Up, up ! Ye dames and lasses gay !
To the meadows trip away.
'Tis you must tend the flocks this morn,
And scare the small birds from the corn
Not a soul at home may stay :

For the shepherds must go
With lance and bow
To hunt the wolf in the woods to-day.

Leave the hearth and leave the house
To the cricket and the mouse :
Find grannam out a sunny seat,
With babe and lambkin at her feet.
Not a soul at home may stay :
For the shepherds must go
With lance and bow
To hunt the wolf in the woods to-day.

S. T. COLERIDGE

15. FAIRY LANGUAGE

Puck. How now, spirit ; whither wander you ?
Fairy.   Over hill, over dale,
       Thorough bush, thorough briar,
          Over park, over pale,
       Thorough flood, thorough fire,
       I do wander everywhere,
       Swifter than the moon's sphere ;
       And I serve the fairy queen,
       To dew her orbs upon the green ;
       The cowslips tall her pensioners be ;
       In their gold coats spots you see ;
       Those be rubies, fairy favours—
       In those freckles lie their savours ;

I must go seek some dew-drops here,
And hang a pearl in every cowslip's ear.
                    W. SHAKESPEARE

16. FAIRY SONG

SHED no tear !   O ! Shed no tear !
The flower will bloom another year.
Weep no more !   O ! Weep no more !
Young buds sleep in the root's white core.
Dry your eyes ! O ! Dry your eyes !
For I was taught in Paradise
To ease my breast of melodies—
                    Shed no tear.

Overhead !   Look ove rhead !
'Mong the blossoms white and red—
Look up, look up.   I flutter now
On this flush pomegranate bough.
See me !   'Tis this silvery bill
Ever cures the good man's ill.
Shed no tear !   O ! Shed no tear !
The flower will bloom another year.
Adieu, Adieu !—I fly, adieu,
I vanish in the heaven's blue—
                    Adieu, Adieu !
                    J. KEATS

17. The Fairy Queen

Come follow, follow me,
You fairy elves that be :
Which circle on the greene,
Come follow Mab your queene.
Hand in hand let's dance around,
For this place is fairye ground.

When mortals are at rest,
And snoring in their nest ;
Unheard, and unespy'd,
Through key-holes we do glide ;
Over tables, stools, and shelves,
We trip it with our fairy elves.

And if the house be swept,
And from uncleanness kept,
We praise the houshold maid,
And duely she is paid :
For we use before we goe
To drop a tester in her shoe.

Upon a mushroome's head
Our table-cloth we spread ;
A grain of rye, or wheat,
Is manchet, which we eat ;
Pearly drops of dew we drink
In acorn cups fill'd to the brink.

The brains of nightingales,
With unctuous fat of snailes,
Between two cockles stew'd,
Is meat that's easily chew'd;
Tailes of wormes, and marrow of mice,
Do make a dish that's wondrous nice.

The grasshopper, gnat, and fly,
Serve for our minstrelsie;
Grace said, we dance a while,
And so the time beguile:
And if the moon doth hide her head,
The gloe-worm lights us home to bed.

On tops of dewie grasse
So nimbly do we passe;
The young and tender stalk
Ne'er bends when we do walk:
Yet in the morning may be seen
Where we the night before have been.

18. When Green Leaves Come Again

O WHERE do fairies hide their heads
When snow lies on the hills,
When frost has spoiled their mossy beds,
And crystallised their rills ?
Beneath the moon they cannot trip
In circles o'er the plain,
And draughts of dew they cannot sip
Till green leaves come again.

Perhaps in small blue diving-bells
They plunge beneath the waves,
Inhabiting the wreathèd shells
That lie in coral caves,
Perhaps in red Vesuvius
Carousal they maintain ;
And cheer their little spirits thus
Till green leaves come again.

Or maybe in soft garments rolled,
In hollow trees they lie,
And sing when nestled from the cold
To while the season by.
There while they sleep in pleasant trance,
'Neath mossy counterpane,
In dreams they weave some fairy dance
Till green leaves come again.

When they return there will be mirth
And music in the air,
And fairy rings upon the earth,
And mischief everywhere.
The maids, to keep the elves aloof,
Will bar the doors in vain ;
No key-hole will be fairy-proof
When green leaves come again.

                              T. H. BAYLY

19. FAIRIES' RECALL

WHILE the blue is richest
In the starry sky,
While the softest shadows
On the green sward lie,
While the moonlight slumbers
In the lily's urn,
Bright elves of the wild wood !
Oh !   Return, return !

Round the forest fountains,
On the river shore,
Let your silvery laughter
Echo yet once more,
While the joyous boundary
Of your dewy feet
Rings to that old chorus :
" The daisy is so sweet ! "

Oberon, Titania,
Did your starlight mirth
With the song of Avon
Quit this work-day earth ?
Yet while green leaves glisten
And while bright stars burn,
By that magic memory,
Oh !   Return, return.

F. D. HEMANS

The song of Avon refers to the writings of William
Shakespeare, who was born at Stratford-on-Avon and
wrote a play called *A Midsummer Night's Dream* about
the fairies.

20. FLOWERS

SPAKE full well, in language quaint and olden,
One who dwelleth by the castled Rhine,
When he called the flowers, so blue and
    golden,
Stars, that in earth's firmament do shine.

Stars they are, wherein we read our history,
As astrologers and seers of eld ;
Yet not wrapped about with awful mystery,
Like the burning stars, which they beheld.

Wondrous truths, and manifold as wondrous,
God hath written in those stars above;
But not less in the bright flowerets under us
Stands the revelation of his love.

H. W. LONGFELLOW.

21. A Field Flower

There is a flower, a little flower,
With silver crest and golden eye,
That welcomes every changing hour,
And weathers every sky.

The prouder beauties of the field
In gay but quick succession shine—
Race after race their honours yield,
They flourish and decline.

But this small flower, to Nature dear,
While moons and stars their courses run,
Wreathes the whole circle of the year,
Companion of the sun.

It smiles upon the lap of May,
To sultry August spreads its charms,
Lights pale October on his way,
And twines December's arms.

The purple heath and golden broom
On moory mountains catch the gale,
O'er lawns the lily sheds perfume,
The violet in the vale.

But this bold floweret climbs the hill,
Hides in the forest, haunts the glen,
Plays on the margin of the rill,
Peeps down the fox's den.

Within the garden's cultured round
It shares the sweet carnation's bed,
And blooms on consecrated ground
In honour of the dead.

The lambkin crops its crimson gem,
The wild bee murmurs on its breast,
The blue-fly bends its pensile stem
Light o'er the sky-lark's nest.

'Tis Flora's [1] page.   In every place,
In every season, fresh and fair,
It opens with perennial grace,
And blossoms everywhere.

On waste and woodland, rock and plain,
Its humble buds unheeded rise ;
The Rose has but a summer reign,—
The Daisy never dies.

J. MONTGOMERY

22. THE FOOLISH HAREBELL

A HAREBELL hung her wilful head :
" I am tired, so tired !   I wish I was dead."

She hung her head in the mossy dell :
" If all were over, then all were well ! "

[1] *Flora.*   The goddess of the flowers.

The Wind, he heard, and was pitiful,
And waved her about to make her cool.

" Wind, you are rough ! " said the dainty
    Bell ;
" Leave me alone—I am not well."

The Wind, at the word of the drooping dame,
Sighed to himself and ceased in shame.

" I am hot, so hot ! " she moaned and said :
I am withering up ; I wish I was dead ! "

Then the Sun he pitied her woeful case,
And drew a thick veil over his face.

" Cloud, go away, and don't be rude,"
She said ; " I do not see why you should ! "

The Cloud withdrew.   Then the Harebell cried,
" I am faint, so faint !—and no water beside ! "

The Dew came down its millionfold path :
She murmured, " I did not want a bath ! "

The Dew went up ; the Wind softly crept ;
The Night came down, and the Harebell slept.

A boy ran past in the morning gray,
Plucked the Harebell, and threw her away.

The Harebell shivered and sighed, " Oh ! Oh !
I am faint indeed !   Come, dear Wind, blow."

The Wind blew gently, and did not speak,
She thanked him kindly, but grew more weak.

" Sun, dear Sun, I am cold ! " she said.
He shone ; but lower she drooped her head.

" O Rain, I am withering !   All the blue
Is fading out of me !—come, please do ! "

The Rain came down as fast as he could,
But for all his good-will he could do her no
        good.

She shuddered and shrivelled, and moaning
        said,
" Thank you all kindly ! " and then she was
        dead.

Let us hope, let us hope when she comes
        next year,
She'll be simple and sweet ! But I fear, I
        fear !

G. MACDONALD

23. LILIES

WE are lilies fair,
The flower of virgin light ;
Nature held us forth, and said,
" Lo ! my thoughts of white ! "

Ever since then, angels
Hold us in their hands ;
You may see them where they take
In pictures their sweet stands.

Like the garden's angels
Also do we seem,
And not the less for being crowned
With a golden dream.

Could you see around us
The enamoured air,
You would see it pale with bliss
To hold a thing so fair.

LEIGH HUNT

24. THE ROSE

THE rose had been wash'd, just wash'd in a
    shower,
Which Mary to Anna conveyed ;
The plentiful moisture encumber'd the flower,
And weigh'd down its beautiful head.

The cup was all fill'd, and the leaves were all
    wet,
And it seem'd, to a fanciful view,
To weep for the buds it had left with regret
On the flourishing bush where it grew.

I hastily seized it, unfit as it was
For a nosegay, so dripping and drown'd,
And swinging it rudely, too rudely, alas !
I snapp'd it, it fell to the ground.

" And such," I exclaimed, " is the pitiless part
Some act by the delicate mind,
Regardless of wringing and breaking a heart
Already to sorrow resign'd.

" This elegant rose, had I shaken it less,
Might have bloom'd with its owner awhile ;
And a tear that is wiped with a little address,
May be follow'd perhaps by a smile."

W. COWPER

25. THE VIOLET

DOWN in a green and shady bed,
    A modest violet grew,
Its stalk was bent, it hung its head
    As if to hide from view.

G

And yet it was a lovely flower,
   Its colours bright and fair ;
It might have graced a rosy bower,
   Instead of hiding there.

Yet there it was content to bloom,
   In modest tints arrayed ;
And there diffused its sweet perfume,
   Within the silent shade.

Then let me to the valley go,
   This pretty flower to see ;
That I may also learn to grow
   In sweet humility.

                J. TAYLOR

26. THE LITTLE THIRSTY LILY

LITTLE white Lily
Sat by a stone,
Drooping and waiting,
Till the sun shone.
Little white Lily
Sunshine has fed ;
Little white Lily
Is lifting her head.

Little white Lily
Said, " It is good :

Little white Lily's
Clothing and food !
Little white Lily
Drest like a bride !
Shining with whiteness,
And crowned beside ! "

Little white Lily
Droopeth in pain,
Waiting and waiting
For the wet rain.
Little white Lily
Holdeth her cup :
Rain is fast falling,
And filling it up.

Little white Lily
Said, " Good again,
When I am thirsty
To have nice rain !
Now I am stronger,
Now I am cool ;
Heat cannot burn me,
My veins are so full ! "

Little white Lily
Smells very sweet :
On her head sunshine,
Rain at her feet.

Thanks to the sunshine !
Thanks to the rain !
Little white Lily
Is happy again ! "

G. MACDONALD

27. THE ARROW AND THE SONG

I SHOT an arrow into the air,
It fell to earth, I knew not where ;
For, so swiftly it flew, the sight
Could not follow it in its flight.

I breathed a song into the air,
It fell to earth, I knew not where ;
For who has sight so keen and strong,
That it can follow the flight of song ?

Long, long afterward, in an oak
I found the arrow, still unbroke ;
And the song, from beginning to end,
I found again in the heart of a friend.

H. W LONGFELLOW

28. THE DOG AND THE WATER-LILY

THE noon was shady, and soft airs
    Swept Ouse's silent tide,
When, 'scaped from literary cares,
    I wander'd on his side.

My spaniel, prettiest of his race,
    And high in pedigree,
(Two nymphs adorn'd with every grace
    That spaniel found for me).

Now wanton'd lost in flags and reeds,
    Now starting into sight,
Pursued the swallow o'er the meads
    With scarce a slower flight.

It was the time when Ouse display'd
    His lilies newly blown ;
Their beauties I intent survey'd,
    And one I wish'd my own.

With care extended far I sought
    To steer it close to land ;
But still the prize, though nearly caught,
    Escaped my eager hand.

Beau, mark'd my unsuccessful pains
    With fix'd considerate face,

And puzzling set his puppy brains
    To comprehend the case.

But with a cherup clear and strong
    Dispersing all his dream ;
I thence withdrew, and follow'd long
    The windings of the stream.

My ramble ended I return'd ;
    Beau, trotting far before,
The floating wealth again discern'd,
    And plunging left the shore.

I saw him with that lily cropp'd,
    Impatient swim to meet
My quick approach, and soon he dropp'd
    The treasure at my feet.

Charm'd with the sight, " The world," I cried,
    " Shall hear of this thy deed :
My dog shall mortify the pride
    Of man's superior breed.

" But chief myself I will enjoin,
    Awake at duty's call,
To show a love as prompt as thine
    To Him who gives me all."

                  W COWPER

29. ELDORADO

GAILY bedight
A gallant knight,
In sunshine and in shadow,
    Had journeyed long,
    Singing a song,
In search of Eldorado.

    But he grew old—
    This knight so bold—
And o'er his heart a shadow
    Fell as he found
    No spot of ground

That looked like Eldorado.
    And, as his strength
    Failed him at length,
He met a pilgrim shadow—
    " Shadow," said he,
    " Where can it be—
" This land of Eldorado ? "

    " Over the Mountains
    Of the Moon,
Down the valley of the Shadow,
    Ride, boldly ride,"
    The shade replied.
" If you seek for Eldorado ! "

E. A. POE

Eldorado. El Dorado (which in Spanish means " the
gilded one ") was a name given first to the chief of a
South American tribe, and afterwards to an imaginary
country rich in gold.

30. Lilian

Airy, fairy Lilian,
    Flitting, fairy Lilian,
When I ask her if she love me,
Claps her tiny hands above me,
    Laughing all she can ;
She'll not tell me if she love me,
    Cruel little Lilian.

When my passion seeks
    Pleasance in love-sighs,
She, looking thro' and thro' me
Thoroughly to undo me,
    Smiling, never speaks :
So innocent-arch, so cunning simple,
From beneath her gathered wimple
    Glancing with black-beaded eyes,
Till the lightning laughters dimple
    The baby-roses in her cheeks ;
    Then away she flies.

Prythee weep, May Lilian !
    Gaiety without eclipse
Wearieth me, May Lilian :
Thro' my very heart it thrilleth
    When from crimson-threaded lips
Silver-treble laughter trilleth :
Prythee weep, May Lilian.

Praying all I can,
If prayers will not hush thee,
  Airy Lilian,
Like a rose-leaf I will crush thee,
  Fairy Lilian.

LORD TENNYSON

31. THE MERMAID

I

WHO would be
A mermaid fair,
Singing alone,
Combing her hair
Under the sea,
In a golden curl
With a comb of pearl,
On a throne ?

II

I would be a mermaid fair ;
I would sing to myself the whole of the day ;
With a comb of pearl I would comb my hair ;
And still as I comb'd I would sing and say,
" Who is it loves me ? Who loves not me ? "
I would comb my hair till my ringlets would
      fall

Low adown, low adown,
From under my starry sea-bud crown
Low adown and around,
And I should look like a fountain of gold
Springing alone
With a shrill inner sound
Over the throne,
In the midst of the hall ;
Till that great sea-snake under the sea
From his coiled sleeps in the central deeps
Would slowly trail himself sevenfold,
Round the hall where I sate, and look in at
the gate
With his large calm eyes for the love of me
And all the mermen under the sea
Would feel their immortality
Die in their hearts for the love of me.

LORD TENNYSON

32. THE MERMAN

I

WHO would be,
A merman bold,
Sitting alone,
Singing alone,
Under the sea,
With a crown of gold,
On a throne ?

II

I would be a merman bold,
I would sit and sing the whole day long ;
I would fill the sea-halls with a voice of power ;
But at night I would roam abroad and play
With the mermaids in and out of the rocks,
Dressing their hair with the white sea-flower ;
And holding them back by their flowing locks
I would kiss them often under the sea,
And kiss them again, till they kiss'd me
    Laughingly, laughingly ;
And then we would wander away, away
To the pale-green sea-groves straight and high,
    Chasing each other merrily.

III

There would be neither moon nor star ;
But the wave would make music above us
    afar—
Low thunder and light in the magic night–
    Neither moon nor star.
We would call aloud in the dreamy dells,
Call to each other and whoop and cry
    All night merrily, merrily ;
They would pelt me with starry spangles and
    shells,
Laughing and clapping their hands between,
    All night, merrily, merrily ;

But I would throw to them back in mine
Turkis [1] and agate and almondine, [2]
Then leaping out upon them unseen
I would kiss them often under the sea,
And kiss them again till they kiss'd me
    Laughingly, laughingly.
Oh ! what a happy life were mine
Under the hollow-hung ocean green !
Soft are the moss-beds under the sea ;
We would live merrily, merrily.

                LORD TENNYSON

33. I HAD A DOVE

I HAD a dove, and the sweet dove died ;
And I have thought it died of grieving ;
O, what could it grieve for ?   Its feet were tied
With a ribbon thread of my own hand's weaving.
Sweet little red feet !   Why should you die ?
Why would you leave me, sweet bird !   Why ?
You lived alone in the forest tree :
Why, pretty thing, would you not live with
    me ?
I kissed you oft and gave you white peas ;
Why not live sweetly, as in the green trees ?

                J. KEATS

---

[1] *Turkis.*   The turquoise.

[2] *Almondine* (or Almandine).   A precious stone of deep red colour.

34. Long Ago

I ONCE knew all the birds that came
    And nested in our orchard trees,
For every flower I had a name,—
    My friends were woodchucks,[1] toads, and
        bees;
I knew where thrived in yonder glen
    What plants would soothe a stone-bruised
        toe—
Oh, I was very learned then,
    But that was very long ago.

I knew the spot upon the hill
    Where checker-berries [2] could be found,
I knew the rushes near the mill
    Where pickerel [3] lay that weighed a pound !
I knew the wood—the very tree
    Where lived the poaching, saucy crow,
And all the woods and crows knew me—
    But that was very long ago.

And pining for the joys of youth,
    I tread the old familiar spot,
Only to learn this solemn truth
    I have forgotten, am forgot.

[1] *Woodchucks.* A burrowing quadruped, resembling the marmot.

[2] *Checker-berries.* The fruit of the American wintergreen.

[3] *Pickerel.* Small pike

Yet here's this youngster at my knee
  Knows all the things I used to know ;
To think I once was wise as he !—
  But that was very long ago.

I know it's folly to complain
  Of whatsoe'er the fates decree,
Yet, were not wishes all in vain,
  I tell you what my wish should be :
I'd wish to be a boy again,
  Back with the friends I used to know.
For I was, oh, so happy then—
  But that was very long ago !

Eugene Field

35. If I had but two little wings

If I had but two little wings
And were a little feathery bird,
    To you I'd fly, my dear !
But thoughts like these are idle things,
    And I stay here.

But in my sleep to you I fly :
I'm always with you in my sleep !
    The world is all one's own.
But then one wakes, and where am I ?
    All, all alone.

Sleep stays not, though a monarch bids :
So I love to wake 'ere break of day :
    For though my sleep be gone,
Yet while 'tis dark, one shuts one's lids,
    And still dreams on.
S. T. COLERIDGE

36. THE WATER-NYMPH AND THE BOY

    I FLUNG me round him,
    I drew him under ;
    I clung, I drown'd him,
    My own white wonder ! . . .

    Father and mother,
      Weeping and wild,
    Came to the forest,
      Calling the child.
    Came from the palace,
      Down to the pool,
    Calling my darling,
      My beautiful !
    Under the water,
      Cold and so pale,
    Could it be love made
      Beauty to fail ?

    Ah me for mortals !
      In a few moons,

If I had left him
  After some Junes
He would have faded,
  Faded away,
He, the young monarch, whom
  All would obey,
  Fairer than day :
Alien to springtime,
  Joyless and gray,
He would have faded,
  Faded away,
Moving a mockery,
  Scorn'd of the day !

Now I have taken him
  All in his prime,
Saved from slow poisoning
  Pitiless Time,
Fill'd with his happiness,
  One with the prime,
Saved from the cruel
  Dishonour of Time.
Laid him, my beautiful,
  Laid him to rest,
Loving, adorable,
  Softly to rest,
Here in my crystalline,
  Here in my breast !

HON. R. NOEL

37. THE NIGHT BIRD

A FLOATING, a floating
Across the sleeping sea,
All night I heard a singing bird
Upon the topmost tree.

" Oh !   Came you off the isles of Greece,
Or off the banks of Seine ;
Or off some tree in forests free,
Which fringe the western main ? "

" I came not off the old world
Nor yet from off the new—
But I am one of the birds of God
Which sing the whole night through."

" Oh sing, and wake the dawning—
Oh whistle for the wind ;
The night is long, the current strong,
My boat it lags behind."

" The current sweeps the old world,
The current sweeps the new ;
The wind will blow, the dawn will glow,
Ere thou hast sailed them through."

C. KINGSLEY

H

38. Let Me Rest

He does well who does his best :
Is he weary ?   Let him rest :
Brothers !   I have done my best,
I am weary—let me rest.
After toiling oft in vain,
Baffled, yet to struggle fain ;
After toiling long, to gain
Little good with mickle pain ;
Let me rest—but lay me low,
Where the hedge-side roses blow ;
Where the little daisies grow,
Where the winds a-maying go ;
Where the footpath rustics plod ;
Where the breeze-bowed poplars nod ;
Where the old woods worship God ;
Where His pencil paints the sod ;
Where the wedded throstle sings ;
Where the young bird tries his wings ;
Where the wailing plover swings ;
Near the runlet's rushy springs ;
Where, at times the tempest's roar,
Shaking distant sea and shore,
Still will rave old Barnesdale o'er,
To be heard by me no more !
There, beneath the breezy west,
Tired and thankful, let me rest,
Like a child, that sleepeth best,
On its gentle mother's breast.

E. Elliot

39. HIAWATHA'S CHILDHOOD

AT the door on Summer evenings
Sat the little Hiawatha ;
Heard the whispering of the pine-trees,
Heard the lapping of the water,
Sounds of music, words of wonder ;
" Minne-wawa ! " said the pine-trees,
" Mudway-aushka ! " said the water.
Saw the fire-fly, Wah-wah-taysee,
Flitting through the dusk of evening,
With the twinkle of its candle
Lighting up the brakes and bushes,
And he sang the song of children,
Sang the song Nokomis taught him :
" Wah-wah-taysee, little fire-fly,
Little, flitting, white-fire insect,
Little, dancing, white-fire creature,
Light me with your little candle,
Ere upon my bed I lay me,
Ere in sleep I close my eyelids ! "
Saw the moon rise from the water,
Rippling, rounding from the water,
Saw the flecks and shadows on it,
Whispered, " What is that, Nokomis ? "
And the good Nokomis answered :
" Once a warrior, very angry,
Seized his grandmother, and threw her
Up into the sky at midnight ;
Right against the moon he threw her ;

'Tis her body that you see there."
Saw the rainbow in the heaven,
In the eastern sky the rainbow,
Whispered, " What is that, Nokomis ? "
And the good Nokomis answered :
" 'Tis the heaven of flowers you see there ;
All the wild-flowers of the forest,
All the lilies of the prairie,
When on earth they fade and perish,
Blossom in that heaven above us."
When he heard the owls at midnight,
Hooting, laughing in the forest,
" What is that ? " he cried in terror,
" What is that ? " he said, " Nokomis ? "
And the good Nokomis answered :
" That is but the owl and owlet,
Talking in their native language,
Talking, scolding at each other."
Then the little Hiawatha
Learned of every bird its language,
Learnt their names and all their secrets,
How they built their nests in summer,
Where they hid themselves in winter,
Talked with them whene'er he met them,
Called them " Hiawatha's Chickens."

H. W. LONGFELLOW

www.ingramcontent.com/pod-product-compliance
Ingram Content Group UK Ltd.
Pitfield, Milton Keynes, MK11 3LW, UK
UKHW012327130625
459647UK00009B/120